THE
FOLD

A Collection of Poetry

La Shawn Courtwright

PAGE PUBLISHING, INC.
New York, NY

First originally published by Page Publishing, Inc. 2019

ISBN 978-1-64462-006-9 (Paperback)
ISBN 978-1-64462-007-6 (Digital)

Printed in the United States of America

OUTSIDER

I'm an outsider
Cause er'thing I do
is on the outside.

Jus like when I think
it's on the outside.

Even if I drink,
I'm on the brink
of the outside.

When I tell people
what's on my mind,
it's on the outside.

My life,
I have lived it
on the outside.

My goals and dreams
linger
on the outside.

Even my writing's
on the outside.

More so,
my poetry
speaks
to the outside.

My destiny
is on the outside
of what some people
thought it would be.

I'm so outside; my mind,
that that's where I'm
free.

Outside of you, only
from the inside
to the outside,
that's what makes
me, me.

Outsiders are not
conformist
and constrained by
society.

I live
the outsider
liberty.
OUTSIDE!

THE FOLD

I've waited so many years
for the day that my sheep
would come back to the fold.

I could see it coming soon,
for it borders upon a new horizon.
At last, I've found almost all of my babies.
Alas, you all may return home.

Never should have happened.
Although, many times,
didn't know how I was gonna make it.
What gave them the right to
take them,
those,
MINE!

When they were in the fold,
My three sweet, loving, gentle sheep
Didn't see the wolves that lay
around,
near.
They had stood at our feet.

I thought that they were safe and secure.
Obvious now,
then, I was oblivious to traitors.
They had me faded,
blindsided by their demure.

I've got my ideas
Until the good Lord reveals the truth,
I can never be sure.
It was a tragic era in our lives,
cutting pain
as if constantly being stuck with
knives.

The many days I could not keep the tears
from flowing,
not knowing
where my sheep were.
If they were alive and well,
What an everyday livin' hell.

Having to accept this shit,
not knowing.
For the sake of them,
My sheep,
I didn't do what I wanted to do
to those responsible,
had their stake in my innocent sheep
going.

For the bitter seeds that are reaped
of this,
these sorts of thoughts,
I would have become lower even than them,
were not worth sowing.

Hang in there Shawn,
they'll be back one day.
Each one of them, for you to hold,
Won't get a chance to steal my sheep,
any more wolves.
They've come back to the fold.

I'D NEVER LET A MAN HAVE
THAT KINDA POWER OVER ME

Very—so ever temptin'—his touch
I should have known, when I tasted, or his love,
bittersweet.
Don't know how I found myself in the throes of his depths.
Somethin' insida me didn't want to help itself.
Layin' soft, tender kisses all over me.
Thought I had it all.
Seemed like the world was at my feet.
I'd never let a man have that kinda power over me!

Said he'd had his eyes on me.

This,
I don't know for how long.
All I know is, seemed like destiny
had come to me to behold.
In his arms, I'd lay, his strength,
not just physical in his body.
He knew he had the ability.
My mind and body were his for the taking.
He readily possessed of them;
the way he did, I was his mold.
At that time, if I could have,
to him, my soul I would have bequeathed.
I'd never let a man have that kinda power over me!

I was so rapt; I went anywhere he would lead.
So blinded by what he was givin' me.
Somethin' even higher than pure ecstasy.
He was just there to capture my heart.
Yes! He did leave.
But not before with me, he had planted his seed.
Her name is Ennocence.
His was never love for me.
The love I had for him has been tainted.
He broke my heart; his promise of matrimony.
I'd never let a man have that kinda power over me!

Not Helpless, or Hopeless, Just Homeless

Men, women, and children nowadays
find themselves deeply infused
in this thing we call "homelessness."

When people see us about
doing what we can to make it through the day,
not understanding the circumstances,
people meet our eyes,
their faces full of disdain!

We're not helpless or hopeless,
just under a bit of a strain
of the constantly changing economy,
in which for now we remain.

We can all bring this to a halt.
This thing called "homelessness"!
That is to stop any further despair.
With this in mind, we're only merely
there!

Homelessness is not a disease,
you don't catch it like a common cold
from a sneeze.

It can come at a time when life is good,
then turn around
like a derailed train, that at
the start, traveling smoothly about the tracks.

Situations hit us and knock us down
like a boxer in a bout,
knocked down in the first round,
flat on his back!

DIFFERENT, BUT HERE

When I look around,
All I can feel
is compassion for all
in this room.

No matter what our
circumstances are,
We share a common thread.
At night, we lay down,
and in the morning,
we rise from the same
blue beds.

All of us with an
expiration date
that represents the end
of our sentence here.

After this, back to the
same lives, or walk
on different paths
other than what
brought us here.

Something, somewhere,
went wrong, seems
to be the only thing
that's clear.

CROSS ARTIST

I was there for you.
Why? How do you choose not
to be here for me?

This was our second try.
Once again, you lied.

You've proven to be contrary
to what you say
and proved you'll always
be a cheat.

I almost cried,
but instead

I dried my eyes.
See,
I'm not the same woman you met initially.

All you will do
is bring me down.

Trying to make a go
of me and you.

I'm choosing not to frown.

You see,
I've decided to pick up
and wear my crown.
I'm more valuable
than that you've dealt me.

You are out of my sight,
out of my mind
and of your bullshit.
I'm free!

No more being hung out
to dry.

What was I thinking?

For that question,
there's not one
reasonable alibi.

I know why you wanted me.

It's because my heart is true.
I refuse to let you
beat it up and turn
it black and blue.

Thank GOD,
once and for all,
I'M DONE WITH YOU!

I'm Going on From Here

Lift me up, oh Lord,
Out of this great abyss!
For I sense there awaits better
things in the outer world.
An awaiting bliss!
Deep from within my heart comes
the inspiration to write!
So my life from out of despair
take flight!
Send your angels to guard
over me!
So that I may do your will,
live upright!
So long, I have suffered tragedy,
Urban blight!
Not only me,
my sons' and daughters' lives
have been crushed
By vicious circles of
beings.
[By a so-called justice system
run amok]
Oh, Lord,
how did we get here?
I don't know the answers
to say such!
Inferior I am in their minds
is how they deem me!
Imperial as I am in God's eye,

But what they think,
HIS plan for me says their labels
never stuck!
I'm
   Going
       On
          From
              Here!

RAINDROP JAIL CELL

There's two shades of dark in this jail cell
full of gloom.

The light switch has two settings,
     one bright, one dim, amid this gloom.
None is the light of the sun.
As you sit, and the time passes, ebbs away.
The only true thing close to you
     is the despair of loneliness, isolated
from everything you love in the outer world.
Even a visit is not face-to-face.
     A video screen monitor,
Broken voices as the technology fails
     to get your message to
the image on the screen.
No hope to touch the ones, in which
so much for them, you so care.
     You'd have to be here to know what I mean.
I heard it raining, the thunder from the storm.
Light flashing through my grayed-out windows
That won't enable me to see a thing.

Yet, I could see that raindrop clearly,
     It's as if God was crying with me.

ARTICLE TO MY MOTHER

A mother's love
Is a many treasured thing.
And onto her love
I cling.
To hear her voice
And see her face
Bring much joy to
My heart.
I never want to,
From her heart, be apart.
She loved me before I knew
How to love myself.
I place her love first
'Cause it's like nothing else.
A mother's love
Is unique in kind.
When I'm goin' through somethin',
My dear mother's teachings come to mind.
That's why a mother's love
Is unique,
Like nothing to it
Can compare.
I love my mom,
And for her,
I'll always be there.
Thank you, Mom,
For your loving,
Caring WAY.
To you, for that,
I wish you a
Happy Mother's Day!

I "AM" WOMAN

I "am" woman,
great as herself,
beyond any of my wants.
I "am" woman, even before my needs.

I "am" woman,
immaculate at time
of my own conception.

I "am" woman
as I gave birth.
I "am" woman, gracious
for my gift to conceive.

I "am" woman, the beauty
given to beseech Mother
Earth with all of the
Wondrous creatures and
things.

I "am" woman, for the
naturalness of the smile
beset on my face,
meant full with joy for
all others willing to receive.

I "am" woman,
each and every day I wake up.
Greeting the days I've lived
to see.

I "am" a great woman.
I "am" a beautiful woman,
every single breath I take,
every single time I breathe!

GOOD ADVICE

Thank you for your good advice.
I'm very honored to have such a direct word;
one which assists me in how I should direct
my own words and use them to help
others!

I feel revived with such vigor, put
forward to perform my tasks.
I'm not afraid anymore.

Now I know I don't have
to put on any particular face,
or hide behind my
masks!

I will use this knowledge so that I may
properly guide my steps.
I'm so gracious for the times when a
little bit of precious time is taken out
for someone like me,
when I needed help.

Thank you for your good advice!

REACH

Reach! Reach!
Up to the heavens high.
Reach! Reach!
Keep your head up.
Reach! Reach!
For the time is nigh.
Reach! Reach!
Only you can do it for yourself.
Yeah! you got the stuff.
Reach! Reach!
You can never give up.
Reach! Reach!
Only you can do it.
Yes, you can. I'm not lying.
Reach! Reach!
You must never stop trying.
The masterpiece is what you create.
You go ahead, do it, demonstrate.
Reach! Reach!
The element of defeat no longer plays a part in my life.
Reach! Reach!

STRENGTH

The emptiness felt of a
broken family and a broken heart.
The loneliness is deeply felt;
however there's strength in
it surprisingly built.

I don't know how I've managed
to strive. Troubled, stressed-out,
didn't have the strength, sometimes,
to make it through.

Somehow, I had the ingenuity
to stay alive! Nearly blew my
mind; the power it took.
I'm so thankful to this, that on
life I'm hooked.

Life's not always what you want it to be.
Stick it out, go with the plan, the
blueprint of what was meant originally.

ABOUT THE AUTHOR

Photo by Peter Beyer

La Shawn Courtwright was born in Detroit, Michigan. In her youth, she was very coy and inward. The one thing she was passionate about was writing. Both her and her writings have transcended. She will permeate the mind, heart, and body of the reader.

She takes the heavy and make it light, said with the tone and effect of her unique laughter because she's very edgy. She will always leave you satisfied with her youthful charisma that shines through in her writings.

Some of her works reflect on victory, hope, tragedy, and numerous truly oppressive devices, both physical and nonphysical, she's experienced in her life. Due to the many forms of oppression, La Shawn Courtwright have endured and overcome, that is why she fearlessly states where she stands on those issues in the flow of her poetry. Her frankness hits so close to home that it prompts her audience to keep turning the pages for more and more.

Ultimately, Courtwright aspires to be amongst the most extraordinary screenwriters in these times. She is an open listener, and many have shared their stories of tyranny with her. She is a true visionary and sees ways to elevate, strengthen, and ease the mind. She's also compassionate and cares for others. Courtwright feels that her livings not in vain, continuing to tell her story and those of others.

She admires her mother for inviting her to her life's milk, reading and writing. She thanks and is grateful for all of her mentors, who've embraced and currently continue to believe in her.

CPSIA information can be obtained
at www.ICGtesting.com
Printed in the USA
BVHW070918101220
594978BV00005B/81